The Unknowing Muse

Poems

by

SARAH WHITE

*For Sue
in Art and Friendship —
Warmly,
Sarah*

DOS MADRES

2014

DOS MADRES PRESS INC.

P.O.Box 294, Loveland, Ohio 45140

www.dosmadres.com   editor@dosmadres.com

Dos Madres is dedicated to the belief that the small press is essential
to the vitality of contemporary literature as a carrier of the new voice,
as well as the older, sometimes forgotten voices of the past. And in an
ever more virtual world, to the creation of fine books pleasing to the
eye and hand.

Dos Madres is named in honor of Vera Murphy and Libbie Hughes,
the "Dos Madres" whose contributions have made this press possible.

Dos Madres Press, Inc. is an Ohio Not For Profit Corporation and a
501 (c) (3) qualified public charity. Contributions are tax deductible.

Executive Editor: Robert J. Murphy

Illustration & Book Design: Elizabeth H. Murphy
www.illusionstudios.net
Cover: "The Divine Sarah Bernhardt" by Sarah White

Typset in Adobe Garamond Pro & Aquiline
ISBN 978-1-939929-15-0
Library of Congress Control Number: 2014941812

First Edition

ACKNOWLEDGEMENTS

I am grateful to the editors of the following publications in which these poems appear, or are forthcoming:

Good Works Anthology, (poems to honor Malala Yousafzai), "Of Emilie, who would have known."

Hanging Loose, "My Anonymous Hour" (also in Poetry Daily)

Hotel Amerika, "Duet for Soprano and Baritone"

Lyre, Lyre, "the storm with the silly name," "trooper."

Mystic Nebula, "Spell," "the universe remains simple and strange"

OC (Toulouse), "Two Occitan Poets Lost as in N.Y. I Study Their Language"

Offcourse Literary Review, "From a Paris Journal," "Il pleure...comme il pleut," "Mother-Daughter Excursion," "Memento" "Purgatory Stories," "The Cab Driver Says I Look Like a Teacher," "Victoria De Los Angeles."

PN, "Andrei Zhdanov, Director of the Writers' Union, Reports to Premier Stalin on Anna Akhmatova"

The Lake, "Atlas of Objects, Verbs, and Voices"

The Prose Poem Project, "For Sale, Edwardian Music Box," "The Harp and the Hammer"

Third Wednesday, "Hannah."

Sleet Magazine, "German Spoken Here," "Mrs. Hughes's Bees"

Voices (Institute for Retired Professionals), "Snow Globe at Kennedy Airport in 2004"

Western Humanities Review, "Can a Pen Write the Real," "Completed Actions in the Past," "Fire Can't be Slowed, Only Retold," "Knossos."

for

Eulalia, Nellie,
Marion, Malala,
Emily, Emilie

Table of Contents

III
ANALOGUE

EPILOGUE

PROLOGUE

Posted on the bulletin board at school:
EXPERIENCED TUTOR
AND MUSE

Not a single student calls,
just one of the teachers:.
I'm seeking a Muse.
When I was younger
I learned from my Shadows
and didn't need Daughters of Apollo.

I

The Cab Driver Says I Look Like a Teacher

It must be the drab
down coat I wear, the hair
neither colored nor curled,

the eyes tinged
with inky quizzes
and frown lines

as if the driver
were a writer
and I a character

remembering
a Freshman girl
reciting Verlaine

on her last morning
in the world—*O Marion,*
what have you done?—

remembering Borges
coming to the campus,
and the Dean

coming to my office,
saying I had tenure.
thanking him

and thinking *nobody*
will ever
make love to me again.

Fire Can't Be Slowed, Only Retold

(Bronx, NY, March, 2007)

My kite is blue. I have a blue kite
insists the stick picture
and the date Abudabacary wrote
the day before the night
his time not to exist began.

Flames will get longer
and longer ago
but his place in the room
with the alphabet stays.

Friends say 'Don't Matter'
was his favorite song
but they don't think it is.
He can't still like it.

They still like him. Weird
that he can't
like them back.

For Abudabacary
of Mali, a garden
will be planted in front
while, in the hall,
a picture insists
on holding its string and kite.

Completed Actions in the Past

Examples of the perfect:

> My student has learned a poem by Verlaine.

> She hasn't learned it.

> She has, but something has happened.

The poem has spilled onto the lanes
of a Maryland road—

> O Marion,

what has become of you,
so young?

Lesson and accident perfect, done,

while, incomplete, I'm reading
the poem again.

> *The sky over a roof*
> *is blue and calm.*

"On the Antithetical Meaning of Primal Words"

Freud—old and low-spirited—
acknowledged his fiends
and commended the kindness
of the Gestapo
for sending to London
gifts that were poison
when they were German.

Deities, beauties,
soon to ease death
among his chows and loved women.

Peter Ginz, fourteen and unknown,
became guest in a town
arrayed as a schoolroom,
though a prison.
He shone, hard gem,
a captain of children,
and met his end with them.

O hostile hosts! Who were the flies,
and who the wanton boys?
To overcome distance, what use?

We have a savage language.

Of Emilie, who would have known…

(Newtown, Connecticut, December, 2012)

It's what they knew that makes you wail:
how to tie a shoe, zip a coat,
form an alphabet with magic
markers, have it rhyme. Years ago,

I lost a girl who knew by heart a poem
in a language not her own. I wailed
"Not Marion! Not Marion!" Where
was the poem now that she was gone?

Where's the phrase a child could say
in perfect Portuguese? *Good
Morning Dad—* I'm afraid nobody
says it any more, not even in Brazil,

since we lost Emilie, the only one who
would have known how to console us.

Hannah

She stands on the veranda
in Constant Spring, Jamaica,
beside a tanned
and sturdy widower—
my grandfather.

She's just my height
though I'm a child of ten.
She has a woman's hips
and breasts. Her skin
is like oiled sandalwood.

Loaned to me this afternoon,
she leads me through a garden
to her little house that seems
a house for children
without the games,

only the combs, rings,
embroidered blouses, beaded
necklaces, gifts—all
I'll ever know about her beaux,

and one old man
who will be sending for her soon.

Emily in the Mountains

A cockle shell
a begging bowl

a prayer and hymn
a cap and brim

a map and walk
a staff and stalk

a satchel
and a fitful journal—

All of these—O Pyrenees—
equip my mind.

What Campostela
will I find?

What Pompeii?
Though arbitrary Alps

bar the way,
I can step next door

to see Vesuvian flames
and hear the roar.

Mother-Daughter Excursion

(Paris, 1958)

She ushered me
into the Cluny museum
to view *la ceinture
de chasteté,*

emblem of husbands,
wives, Crusades,
possession.
Was it a joke,
a lesson, or menace
she wanted to offer
her virgin girl
in Paris—one
of the sights—

less belt than girdle,
its canvas panels
cunningly locked,

the artifact—a fake
no longer displayed
along the way

to a round garden, rose and blue,
where the royal unicorn
surrenders to a kind maiden.

Trooper

Something in his posture
makes me wonder if his mother
and father were troopers
who taught him a trooper's
way to occupy the space
between the edge of the road
and the car he just pulled over.

He reminds me of the trooper
at a court in Elkton, Maryland
where I stood beside a teenager
charged with assaulting
that very officer somewhere
near the Pennsylvania border.

A witness to that sorry scene
might have thought the teen
better off with troopers
as parents rather than professors
who loved their son
but no longer loved each other.

Hold Still! or, Ode To the Tattoo Master

From the Northeast
Kingdom to the South
Seas, from Greater Boston
to Lesser Antilles,
wherever your craft is plied,
the Brave wait
to be scarified.

You wrote "Born to Be Brave"
on Eulalia's hip
and, on her shoulder, "Endurance,"
(that wrecked ship).

If I, her grandmother, endure
your inks and sterile instruments,
my forearm will honor
some other disaster.

 "Don't do it, Ma," says Owen.
"It hurts." He should know.

A grown man, he bears
on his back a blood-
red flower. Its thorny stem
slashes into his flesh
and out again. "My son
is lost!" I thought at first. The shock
wore off. The rose did not.

14

Monsieur l'Artiste, I am resigned
to your painstaking,
pain-making trade.

Your pen has stung
my near and dear.
I remain unengraved.

Anecdote of Hunger

I saw a man on the train
sit down in two seats.
A girl of nine
or ten sat down beside him.

His summery blue
and white woven shirt
covered, not the belly
of a man,
but a kettle of soup—
a salty, simmering
broth of affection,
garnished with anxious barley,
turnips of shame
and onions of anger
at someone
other than the girl—
his favorite person
in the world.

At 66th Street,
he stood up, signaled
his companion, adjusted
the weight of the kettle,
and carried it
out the sliding doors,
not spilling a drop.

The car felt cold
and empty.
I moved
into one of his seats.

Mother to Sons

I handed you out the door like puppies
and left you alone

to pop your wheelies,
break your clavicles, take sick

with croup, strep, and impetigo.
A doctor's ultra-violet glow

greened your yellow lesions, blued
your hands like hands of Jumblies

sailing in a home-made sieve,
whirling in eccentric eddies,

wearing ocean charts as hats,
paddling, bailing, sailing

down to Baltimore—
Fait Avenue. I stare

but do not try the door
of the former candy store.

I will send a telegram
that rhymes with who I am.

love, Mom

Remember the Cab Driver and What He Knew

When I heard the Seller of Shoes
speak the very same Truth,
I searched for clues. There was Judy,
my neighbor. When we were five
I taught her to read—the Tale
of the Peach That Gave Birth to a Baby.

There was me at fifteen—
not sleeping late, or learning to flirt.
They assumed I was born to teach.
They gave me a flock of kids and lambs
from nearby farms to lead in a Biblical song:

The Wise Man built his house upon a rock...

The house stood firm.
Judy traveled the world as a diplomat.
I stayed home, an explainer of grammar,
plainer and plainer, forever a teacher.
The Driver knows, and the Seller of Shoes—
To hear him talk,

I tip to one side when I walk.

:

II

TRAVELOGUE

According to Horace,
Those who cross the seas
change the sky and not their minds.

Never mind. Here are diaries
of some journeys.

At Kennedy Airport, 2004

I remove my shoes
and stand until the guard approves—
"Go to your gate."

There's time before my flight
to visit paperweight
cities like the ones
at Orly and De Gaulle
with little Arcs of Triumph
and Eiffel Towers.

Manhattan's
no bigger than my palm—
tiny taxi, sponge-tree, Pepsi sign,
bridge, boat, Miss Liberty,

and the towers
we lost three years ago.
An artisan in China
doesn't know,
or chooses to season
souvenir with oblivion.

I pick it up,
unleash a storm,
and watch the snow
come harm-
lessly down.

From a Paris Journal

Every day, it rains.

I come to Parc Montsouris
to honor Jacques Prévert
who kissed someone in a poem
one winter day
on this Mount of Mice.

I come to Montparnasse.
A man pruning trees directs me—
Là-bas, Madame—Charles
Baudelaire lies between
his mother, Caroline,
and Général Aupick, the stepfather
he couldn't bear.

The poet's friends
have pocked his grave
with pebbles, twigs, sad
plants, and a wine-flask.

Near the main gate,
Sartre and Beauvoir
await their visitors.
Some leave notes,
others, metro tickets.

Damp from the fine rain
called *bruine,*
I walk a long time
to find the Becketts,
Sam and Suzanne.

When I see their names
twinned in the granite
my eyes are confused
by the veins and the sheen

and I come away changed.

*t*he storm with a silly name

crawled up the coast
to prove itself,

shut off the lights
and shrieked to show
it was female,

cleared
its brackish throat
to show it was male,

picked up sharks,
sent them underground
with the drowned trains

to prove it was God,
threw out the toys
and half the local sand

before it veered
inland where
the houses were

and killed
to prove it was not
a child.

Il pleure…comme il pleut

To Verlaine, the sound of tears
resembles the sound of rain
falling on a town where a man
weeps his wasted years
and his heart
breaks into assonance.

In Baudelaire's Paris,
hours of moisture
form languors and humors.

Our climate's different.
Tears and rain
don't rhyme.

Loss befalls us
when dawn is cloudless.

It storms
and we have weddings.

Memento

Sold beside the Seine
for a Euro:

Tour Eiffel a little
taller than a sugar cube
looms over Notre Dame—the spire,
Sacré Coeur—the dome,
Arc de Triomphe too narrow
for a Tomb of the Unknown.

Absent, track of jackboot,
shadow of zeppelin and rocket.

Gone, the guillotine,
gallows,
catacomb.

Oblivion of coats
with a star sewn on.

No flower of evil,
no eternal drizzle.
The town,
shaken, fills
with snow and tinsel.

Sire, the Night is Darker Now

In Brussels,
between the subway
and the Gare Centrale
a tunnel runs.

If you take it
clasp your wallet
in a secret pocket.

Walk directly to the metro
past the buskers
with harmonicas
and hungers,

past the sleepers
under mounded blankets,

past an abandoned rabbit.
Don't approach to stroke it.
The silky ears
could be a trap.

Yesterday was Christmas.
Tonight's the Feast of Stephen.
Someone treks from the song
into the forest

bearing flesh, wine,
kindness.

Reunion in Moissac

Nine when he died, I
was old enough to hold him
in my mind— slender, clean-shaven—
unchanged until now:
      At the Abbey
of Saint Pierre, I meet a kind
old man. His beard, limbs, robe
fall in rhyming waves along the stone,
his oval eyes cast down,
saddened by all he knows.
      In his hand, a coiled scroll
of lamentations:
        My people have forgotten me...Not
        long ago you called me father...

Moving on,
      I meet him once again
seated on a throne. His lap
is like a hammock where
a little soul is rocking
with delight.
      Only now has my father grown
a flowery beard. Only now
does he gather children,
and wrap them in wisdom's napkin.

Knossos

If I would marry him,
he promised,
we'd travel to Knossos.
I thought—

palace acrobats,
King Minos,
his hot queen serviced
by a bull, their monster-
child nursed
in a labyrinth.
I thought—

ingenious Daedalus,
his drowned son
seasoning an ocean.
I thought—

from Minos and the Queen
came Phaedra
who loved frigid,
virtuous Hippolytus.
Thought

designed a maze—a court,
my Crete, my lust,

so I said Yes,
became his spouse,
soon loosed him

and never went to Knossos.

The Doorman and the Dark

My blouse of flowered chiffon has slid
from its hanger and plunged me
head first to the floor of the closet
to grope among the shoes I don't use
and the suitcases I do. Face down
like a downward dog
unable to stand, my thoughts
are of women who fall and
have their bracelets call an ambulance
team that comes and the doorman lets
them in though nobody opened
the door on the morning you…

But that was years ago. I think
now of heads or tails and shoes
I rarely wear. I think of carrying
a suitcase up the steep steps
into a third class train on the hot
route to Rome, the views confused.
I looked for signs to find the names
of towns, supposing I had stopped
in *Uscita* until, at the following
town, the same sign appeared
and pointed to the Exit. I find
the blouse—flowered silk so sheer
I have to wear a camisole.

Allowing my under-limbs to slide
floorward, I push with my hands until
I stand and find a way to hang
the slithery blouse while
downstairs the doorman's
fine but I wouldn't mind meeting
my love in Uscita, the sweetest
of towns.

Letter from Philadelphia, Winter, 1765

It seems a sort of holow day...

She signs it *yr divoted wyf.*
She can't spell.
Few people can.
She writes faithfully and well
to her husband in England
who enjoys the gossip and endearments,
local apples and hand-
made stockings she sends
from the town he's seen just once
in fifteen years.

When the packet boat arrives,
Philadelphia occurs to him
but not for long.
Home is London now.

She's alone.
An ox is a-rosting on the River
and Peple take their plesure
on this winter afternoon.
Light fades from the seasons
and she will not see Benjamin again.
That's what she doesn't say.

Rather, she writes:
It seems a sort of holow day.

Atlas of Objects, Verbs, and Voices

The laws of Intransitive City:

They let you be.
They don't let you have.

You can come
but you can't bring a friend.

You can go up.
You can descend

but your stuff
has to stay in the room.

You can run
as far as you want.

You can sing. Only don't sing a song.
Speak. Only don't say a thing.

***

The Consignment Office

It teems with toys,
trinkets, coins, tickets
spilled from the pockets
of tourists, who check their objects
and seldom return to claim them.

The children they leave
are kept for a week,
then assigned to foster homes
in neighboring counties.
No one returns
to pick them up.
Parents thrive on life
with nothing to lose,
nothing to take to heart.

***

Suburban Scene

Passive on a patio,
curls riffled,
coverlet stirred
by the winds,

no word in her mind,
speech and its parts
unlearned, passion

yet to be undergone,
an infant, wakened
when…

***

Tale of the Transitive Woman:

I have, don't have,
have had, would have,
had had
two sons. One day,
they took off their clothes
and, naked as Saint Francis,
moved to a monastery.

They beg me to join them
in poverty, but I plan to keep
all I have harvested, painted,
written—EARNED,
including my dearest
possession—a mortal disease
whose numerous symptoms require
a different physician for each.

Soon I will call my children. They'll come
and carry me up the Holy Mountain
where mothers and grandmothers go.

As the brothers descend alone
it will snow.

_The universe remains simple and strange_*

(for Bill Rector)

Somewhere an astronomer
receives a picture
from across an unimaginable span
of space and time—
the cosmos in a phase
before it went all spherical
and orbital before matter
in this beautiful oval
was organized as stars comets
planets meteors before the satellite
we know cooled and was divided
by the great distinctions—dark
from light
dry from wet—
to suit amoebas anemones
coral forests warm
water clowns and other reasons
for a snorkel
or telescope to send
an astronomer a picture
of a universe still as simple
and strange as it was before
there were phones
before good or bad
news or numbers on the clock
in a waiting room
to measure whether
any creature no matter
how beloved
will breathe for a greater
or lesser span of hours
than her mother and father.

* _Prof. David N. Spergel, NY TImes, March 22, 2013_

Spell

Moon, by the bright, dry
  vowels of your seas, the dark
  vowels of your oceans,

by *Mà-ria*
  intoned
  like a Polish woman's name

lovely in Latin—
Crisium
Imbrium
Tranquillitatis
circular threesome—

lovely in English—
  Sea of Crises,
  Sea of Rains,
Sea of Tranquility
eternally pocked
by human boots.

Moon,
  promise to keep
  your bodies
  musical,
  waterless, high,
  and visible to my
  naked eye.

PURGATORY STORIES

*I*ntroduction to Purgatory

mountain in the middle of an ocean,

poem in the middle of a poem,
revealed to me a lifetime ago
by a man too famous or too shy
to look his student in the eye.

I want to meet him somewhere
on the mountain
in recovery from Pride or Envy,
but that won't happen.

He'll never be forgiven
for what he did one afternoon
as a widower alone
on his Maryland farm—

took his tractor from the barn,
drove it out beyond the rows
of precious Tuscan vines
into the deepest water of a pond.

The Loneliness of Purgatory

          not for the penitent soul—
it's the island itself

afloat in the Southern Sea
with no neighbors—
no Mallorca, Minorca,
Lesbos, Lemnos,
no spent volcanoes
or boulders cast off
by a friable coast.

Beyond the Gates of Gibraltar
lies nothing but ocean
and this one mountain
with so much to bear—

heavy remorse, forgiveness
in sudden convulsions.
Only the sight of another body
could lighten its burdens.

A Heavy Part of the Story

One friend of mine
used to let his sandy curls
fall along his face
in the manner of an adolescent girl.
Who cares if he was vain
about his hair?
                In time
he'll come to Purgatory,
Terrace Onc,
and plod around the mountain,
shouldering a stone.
                Each living soul
is proud of something—a farm,
a library, a loom, a prize.
On the mountain,
it is weighed
to determine the size
of the load.
                But why
burden my friend at all
when subtle medicines
have changed
the fair young man with curls
into an aging man with none?

40

The Opposite of Sin is Another Sin

Say, Didi of Connecticut, are   you   on the Mountain? It's me,

your former roommate   from Chatham Hall.   I remember how good you were—

all saintly   ambition. I'm the one you   wanted to recruit in your

quest to lose   the Ego and reduce the Self to zero,   though I wondered

what an Ego   would do after God set it loose. One day, you   threw me a dark

look: "Sarah,   you and I had planned to find true Humility at the same   time but

you have   not. How come?" That day, I gave up the pursuit of Virtue.   Now I'm

with the Slothful on the Fourth Terrace. Where the Hell are you?

41

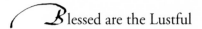B lessed are the Lustful

As a First Responder spends
a minute in the sweet
air to rest, smoke a cigarette,
or speak with a journalist, then
rushes back, joins his friends
and climbs a smoke-filled stair
into harm's way because
harm is what counts, just so,

on the last terrace, a Soul
steps from the flame, speaks a poem
to his Visitor, excuses himself, turns
away, and chooses another hour, day,
or century of fire because the more
he burns the sooner he'll be saved.

News from the Pilgrim

He says he went through Hell,
came out the other side and saw
the stars again.
                    Stars!
He scaled a mountain, rose
through the spheres so far
he was blinded for a while
by *love, sun. and other stars.*
Some finale!
                    My light
comes mostly from the moon.
I've seen the slim moon fatten
and the white moon redden.
I've seen the old moon climb
into the new moon's arms
                            but now
I think about stars all the time.

III

ANALOGUE

The Beatrice Effect

A Girl of nine
turned Beauty, Lady,
Angel, Travel Guide.
A poet held the hem

of her robe and flew
to Heaven for lessons
in her School
of Theology and Optics—

sciences she never learned
in life, hers in the poem
she didn't know he'd write.

I found my own
unknowing muse
when I lost you.

Victoria De Los Angeles

One afternoon, I played an old CD
and let the afternoon be,
along with evening's anticipations
whereupon a bough began
to bend as if the song
were snow—*Du bist die Ruh*,
you are Rest, now lost—
I found myself awash
in thoughts about the man
who died before the man who died
just now, leaving me completely
on my own to resume
missing someone I had missed
all the time without knowing.

All the time, without knowing,
I was thinking I would write
a slim, uneven crown
for him to share with Victoria
De Los Angeles. He had volumes
of her songs, plus a set of blue
World's Classics and a low-
brow collection of pool cues.
I only kept a few of his CD's
and hoped he didn't mind
that I gave most of them away
to a friend who wouldn't be
as sad as I was when he listened,
though I could be wrong.

I could be wrong about the friend,
who doesn't always show,
as I don't always know,
what we're mourning for.
He's the friend to whom
I sold my grand piano.
That was months ago.
I haven't missed it. Something
must be wrong with me,
but let that go and notice
how often I use the word
though—I don't feel at home
though I've lived here for years
and even been loved.

I have even been loved
by the one who left me
on my own to long for someone
else in my odd way, wanting
to ask him if he knew
why Victoria De Los Angeles
sang German songs in Spain
in 1944. *Lieder* are all
very well, but the timing
seems wrong. Victoria was young,
though—21. I was 17 when
I went to Spain, very dumb
about Franco. I just enjoyed
gazpacho, suckling pig, and the Prado.

Gazpacho, suckling pig, and the Prado—
two of which I'm proud
to have sampled—all belong
in this lengthening cycle
on Victoria De Los Angeles.
Whatever the soprano sang in '44
she lived through a Civil War
that could have smothered
a songbird whose mother
was a cleaner, whose father
wasn't powerful either. Who
am I to say Victoria performed
for the dictator? Anyhow,
Catalans have rules of their own.

Catalans have rules of their own
and I might send a crown—
this very one—to Barcelona
where my lover and I never
went together. Oh, we devoted
afternoons to our planned
travels, possibly to Poland
though it never happened.
We only combed every second-
hand bookshop in New England
to complete his blue World's
Classics series. True,
he had dozens at home
but more than one was missing.

More than one was missing
on the winter day I listened
to the songs, and through
a window saw the all
but frozen bough bend
lower and lower under pressure
of the news from Victoria
De Los Angeles. A long,
meandering Kaddish by Ravel
persuaded me that Art
is wise though Rest is lost—
things I knew, ceased
knowing for a time until,
one afternoon, I played an old CD.

Duet for Soprano and Baritone

Madam, Your letter (the signature fictitious, I assume) lay some months unanswered. To respond is no easy task, reluctant as I am, in my declining years, to dampen youthful spirits.

> *Sir, it is an honor to have written you*
> *and received an answer*
> *so considerate in tone, so noble in spirit.*

Madam, Prepare for disappointment. Your admirable Faculty of Verse is all too common nowadays. And writing cannot be the business of a woman, not if she performs her proper work.

> *Painful heat rises to my face*
> *to think of my crude rhapsodies*
> *and quires of paper I have covered*
> *with what once gave me such pleasure!*

You are young, not yet called to women's duties…

> *I am 20, a governess.*
> *I teach or sew, and suppress*
> *the wish to read or write.*

Write, Madam, with no view to celebrity. Write verse for its own sake. Let poetry elevate and calm the mind.

> *I thank you*
> *for allowing me to wield a pen.*
> *Your kind and wise advice shall not be wasted.*

Madam, Farewell…I am your true friend, Robert Southey

> *And I am the authentic C. Bronte.*

Their Alchemy

> begins with a note:
> *I love your verses*
> *with all my heart, Miss Barrett.*

She is afraid. Her suitor's
too young, too strong:
You are Paracelsus. I am a recluse
with nerves...

They meet as rival poets
in contrarious harmony
to speak of prosody
and elopement.

They wait as good Victorians,
taking the heat
through hundreds of tea-times, right
up to the moment of flight:
Tomorrow at this time I shall have you,
only you, to love me.

All is transformed:
She's no longer her father's child.
Without a sound, a spaniel
leaves the house
in his mistress's arms.
The Channel's calm,
the trains on time.
Mistress, master, spaniel,
and lady's maid
travel to Pisa. Soon

a beautiful veil
falls over the honeymoon.

Miss Moore of the Syllables

who "never was known to have fallen in love"
had many a vicious critic: prudes
    upholding their own notion
    of normalcy, and artists
claiming there is no art without turmoil. Meanwhile,

    to her delight, a crow (favored, fabled
creature) became her pet, attracted by
    her beribboned black straw hat.
    She named him Pluto after
the underworld god and what was once considered

    the smallest planet. Was he a tidy bird?
That wasn't a topic for poems.
    He learned to say "Nevermore!"
    but after a while she decided
it was her duty to let him go free. She wrote

    a tender, witty farewell in richly rhymed
Esperanto, went off to Yankee
    Stadium to throw out the first
    pitch of the season—and who
could swear the treasure she'd lost was really a crow?

In Thomas Higginson's Mailbox, April 1862

Sir—
I hope you're not
too deeply occupied —

I have no one to ask—
Father's busy with his briefs.
Mother doesn't care
for thought. The dog
is mute.

You
are an open book—
Send Truth—
Even if it's surgical
I'm thankful.

Tell me:
Do you detect a Breath
in my Verse?

You're not too deeply occupied
I hope.

You don't know me
My name is sealed
in the small envelope.

Mrs. Hughes's Bees

              lacked respect
for genius. They stung
the face and neck

of her husband—brightest,
kindest man in the world!
Later, when he left,
they turned on her.

It happened
at the Devon farm,
once loved and tended,
now bereft.

The kids in their home-
made sunsuits
heard the buzz
and murmur

of bees responding
to Mother's query:
"Is it very stupid
to be happy?"

It is. It is. It is,
Mrs. Hughes.

German Spoken Here

It's a perfect language for children's songs and horror films like Fritz Lang's *M*, where Peter Lorre plays a repulsive predator. "*Ich muss!*" he wails. His round, wide eyes grow wider as he mewls: "Help me! I can do nothing else!"   It's like what Rilke tells a young admirer who wants to know how to become a poet: "Ask yourself whether you *must* create… If you wouldn't die without writing poems, don't write them." *Letters to a Young Poet?* The young man wasn't a poet and never became one. He wasn't one of those actors, adulterers, acrobats, pastors and pianists who claim they make music or havoc in the world because they couldn't do anything else. "I must!" they all say, but it's scarier if they say it in German.

Andrei Zhdanov, Director of the Writers' Union, Reports to Premier Stalin on Anna Akhmatova

She is utterly remote from the People.
She speaks as a unique individual.
Unlike other writers in the capital,
she sings of death, mysticism, doom—

remote from the interests of the People.
Deaf to what is written in her time,
she repeats herself: songs of death,
mysticism and doom

become a blight upon our time
and may corrupt the minds of youth,
the way her verse combines
harlotry with prayer.

Admired by younger minds,
she races frantically between boudoir
and chapel—nun and whore—
she has no concern for the state

only for the boudoir and the chapel.
An overwrought aristocrat
indifferent to the state
and living in the capital

polluting the pages of our journals!
She speaks as a unique individual
unlike other writers.
She is utterly remote from the People.

The Muse Inside

Prisoner Number C-***8,
poet-like, you watch
as a column
of scarlet ants
crosses the concrete
floor of your cell.

Expertly you describe
your overweight, insane
Samoan roommate,
Problem Child,
who smears his shit around
when he's upset.

You have the art
to picture Iceman
Juergens's near-escape,
ending in bullets, gas,
chains, and rape by means
of electric prods.

Who are you, Number C-***8?
You have this skill
and live in hell—
how is that?

What did you do?

Some of us would sell
our souls, or kill,
to write so well.

My Anonymous Hour

opens with a prayer
in prose. I rise: "Hello,
I'm Sarah, and…
I'm a poet."
Hello, Sarah.

"I had an anniversary—
six months without a line."
Applause. "But you know
how it goes—
I wrote a verse
about an adolescent
girl I know (her wanton
clothes). I called it *Schmatta*
and thought it might amuse
her mom and dad,
but they were hurt."

*Have you made amends
to those you harmed?*
I explain my e-mails,
and sit down.

Others stand,
admit to gains
and losses in their fight
against the muse.

We close, schmooze a bit,
depart. The pavement's
full of gaps.

Some of us will slip.

The Marleys of Kingston

(for Hettie Jones)

She lays her mouth on his.
He lays his mouth on hers.
They drink each other's hunger and thirst,
spill songs into each other's mouth.

Alleluia.

He spills daughters and sons.
They all need to be nursed—
the six she bears and a few
whose mothers are strangers.

Alleluia

There are mercies in Babylon—hard work, hits,
a Hope Road house. There are evils—
anger and absence, politics
and guns—he takes his bullet; she takes hers.
It stops short of her brain, trapped in a thicket of dreads.

I and I gonna be all right.

Then, thirsty crab crawls into his foot,
drinks every cell of him
except the Alleluia spilled on his children and all
over the world.

Our Sister's singing still.

Can a Pen Write the Real?

One note repeats
in Chopin's D-flat major Prelude
from its tender salutation
through a C-sharp minor storm that builds,
subsides, returns to major
and resolves—one note
so steady it is usually
called the Raindrop.

Rather than a sound of water, blood,
or word his woman friend
might have harped upon,

rather than the sob
of his own lung, he heard
from deeper in
a music all along
composing *him*
      which dropped
whole
not a prelude to anything.

Practice

I waded, one summer,
      from pool to pool alone,
            read *Magic Mountain*
and climbed a dirt road
      for piano lessons
            with Mr. Pitman,
     a fragile man whose hands,
when not on the keys,
      always trembled.

The Prelude I wanted to learn
      was beyond my skills
            but he didn't mind.
               At season's end
when we said good-bye
      I promised to practice
            over the winter.

But after a while I quit, not
      that I suffered
            from tremors like my teacher.
               I didn't have ruined lungs
            like Chopin or the souls in the novel.
                   I was just too sad to work.
      The winter was dark.

I heard sounds
      of a small harp—
            someone coming—
               but whoever it was
never found me.

For Sale: Edwardian Music Box

Lift the mahogany cover of the six-bell cylinder box. Admire its lush décor—enamel flowers on silvery stems, metal butterflies poised to strike the bells, bells tempered to accompany the tunes, tunes soldered to the surface of the brass drum—which currently won't turn due to a malfunction in the winding gear. We promise to repair it as soon as a buyer is found. Maybe it will be you! The cylinder is sound. There are no broken teeth. When the drum turns again, the teeth will pluck its steel tines, the songs will play, and everything will come back to you—*The Woodland Kiss, The Country Dance, The Love Note, The Flight, The Torn Curtain, The Last Troubadour.*

The Harp and The Hammer

I used to collect harps. Every time I acquired one, I thought it was the harp I'd always wanted, but as I played, I'd realize it wasn't, and put the instrument away with all the rest, each in a white shadow-box that displayed its unique profile.

One day, I wanted a new harp but remembered how the others had lured me with promises of happiness. So, instead of a harp, I got a hammer and smashed the whole collection to bits. For hours, the sprung strings twanged in their ruined houses, making a marvelous din.

Two Occitan Poets Lost as in New York
I Study Their Language

Bernard Manciet (1923-2005)
Max Rouquette (1908-2005)

News is posted on the Web:
Bernard Manciet is dead.
      I never met him,
      haven't read him
yet, but I've read lines
by Max Rouquette
about the spider
      who sets his net
      in a stream of *clar*
      de luna and thinks
      the woven web
      makes constellations
      pale with respect.

Noiseless patient stars
embrace Manciet
tonight. A meteor
ignites the shed
where hens
lay eggs in sweet
straw nests.

Teeth fall out—ripe teeth
      that won't bud

      in the mouth again.
      We needed them

to frame sound
and stop the spills.

The moon sends
no tide this month.

Winds
in a vacant web

weep
Roqueta, Rouquette

EPILOGUE

The Improbables

Opals, not apples, grow in the orchard.
A tooth appears in the mouth of an orchid.
Ocean salt becomes sugar and sweetens
the fish. The rivers return to the mountains.

Dollars flop out of change machines—
the change, too painful, the slots, too narrow.
Arrows cling to their taut bowstrings.
Ammo remains in snug magazines.

A ram shaves his wool and tattoos
the name of a ewe on his skin. A duck
uses one of her plumes as a pen.

I swore I'd forget you when all
these things came to pass. *And none has.*

Your memory greens in me like the grass.

ABOUT THE AUTHOR

 Sarah White studied French and Italian at Harvard and the University of Michigan, specializing in medieval Language and Literature. Before her retirement she was a Professor of French at Franklin and Marshall College in Lancaster, PA. She now lives in New York, writing and painting.

Books by Sarah White

Cleopatra Haunts the Hudson (Spuyten Duyvil, 2007), poetry
> collection

Mrs. Bliss and the Paper Spouses (Pudding House, 2007),
> chapbook

The Poem Has Reasons: a Story of Far Love (Proem Press on-line,
> 2008), lyric memoir

Alice Ages and Ages (BlazeVox, 2010), a sequence of variations

Owen Lewis - *Sometimes Full of Daylight* (2013)

Richard Luftig - *Off The Map* (2006)

Austin MacRae - *The Organ Builder* (2012)

Mario Markus - *Chemical Poems-One For Each Element* (2013)

J. Morris - *The Musician, Approaching Sleep* (2006)

Rick Mullin - *Soutine* (2012), *Coelacanth* (2013)

Robert Murphy - *Not For You Alone* (2004), *Life in the Ordovician* (2007), *From Behind The Blind* (2013)

Pam O'Brien - *The Answer To Each Is The Same* (2012)

Peter O'Leary - *A Mystical Theology of the Limbic Fissure* (2005)

Bea Opengart - *In The Land* (2011)

David A. Petreman - *Candlelight in Quintero - bilingual edition* (2011)

Paul Pines - *Reflections in a Smoking Mirror* (2011), *New Orleans Variations & Paris Ouroboros* (2013), *Fishing on the Pole Star* (2014)

David Schloss - *Behind the Eyes* (2005)

William Schickel - *What A Woman* (2007)

Lianne Spidel & Anne Loveland - *Pairings* (2012), *Bird in the Hand* (2014)

Murray Shugars - *Songs My Mother Never Taught Me* (2011), *Snakebit Kudzu* (2013)

Jason Shulman - *What does reward bring you but to bind you to Heaven like a slave?* (2013)

Olivia Stiffler - *Otherwise, we are safe* (2013)

Carole Stone - *Hurt, the Shadow- the Josephine Hopper poems* (2013)

Nathan Swartzendruber - *Opaque Projectionist* (2009)

Jean Syed - *Sonnets* (2009)

Madeline Tiger - *The Atheist's Prayer* (2010), *From the Viewing Stand* (2011)

James Tolan - *Red Walls* (2011)

Brian Volck - *Flesh Becomes Word* (2013)

Henry Weinfield - *The Tears of the Muses* (2005), *Without Mythologies* (2008), *A Wandering Aramaean* (2012)

Donald Wellman - *A North Atlantic Wall* (2010), *The Cranberry Island Series* (2012)

Anne Whitehouse - *The Refrain* (2012)

Martin Willetts Jr. - *Secrets No One Must Talk About* (2011)

Tyrone Williams - *Futures, Elections* (2004), *Adventures of Pi* (2011)

Kip Zegers - *The Poet of Schools* (2013)

www.dosmadres.com